DON'T BE AN A.S.S. ALL YOUR LIFE

Uncovering The Unconscious Mistakes You Make In Relationships

Shaun D. Upshaw

Don't Be An A.S.S All Your Life

Uncovering The Unconscious Mistakes You Make In Relationships

©Copyright 2014

Shaun D. Upshaw

Editor: Zuleika Abel

For information regarding special discounts for bulk purchases, please contact www.shaunupshaw.com

Dedication

This book is dedicated to all the influential people in my life. Of course, there are too many of you to list, but I want to thank each of you for being so supportive. I want to thank you for allowing me to be me. I want to thank you for believing in me. Words cannot even describe the appreciation I have for each of you.

I also want to dedicate this book to four special ladies in my life. Kendra, Dartha, Amari, and Londin-Taylor, all of you are the foundation that keeps me grounded. The support you give me is beyond words. I love you guys. Your presence alone has propelled me to become a better man and walk in my purpose of changing lives daily.

Table of Contents

ॐ

PREFACE

My views on relationships tend to always lead people toward asking me one particular question: Shaun, where did you gain your relationship insight?

I usually reply with, "Anyone could have my insight if they would just get rid of their ASS mentality. Once I made the decision to not be an ASS any longer, everything pertaining to my relationships became easy to deal with. Outside of that, I believe the transparency to see my mistakes and having vulnerability to express my mistakes is what offers me insight."

You should see the look of confusion on people's faces after I reply in that manner. It is literally hilarious! So instead of continuously giving confusion with my reply, I decided to write this book explaining my insight on just what having an ASS mentality really means. I already know most will not agree with all my relationship views, but it is always good to have an "I told you so" on standby when those people finally do come around. With that said, let's jump right into discussing relationships.

Almost nobody jumps at the opportunity to be transparent and vulnerable concerning relationship mistakes. Why? It's because of **fear**. There you have it, ladies and gentleman! There is the reason why!
It's Fear!

Fear is the one word that keeps you from succeeding in your relationships. It's **fear of hurt**, **fear of rejection**, and **fear of self-exposure** that hinders you. The very thought of fear is the reason you are unable to face yourselves to see the real problem. In fact, it's fear that leaves you in relationship rut after relationship rut. Without a doubt, fear keeps you from transforming into an ideal mate purposed for sustaining a healthy relationship.

Why fear?

Glad you're curious! Listen Up!

Life is a series of events that unfold based on decisions you produce. Each path presented is an opportunity for you to manufacture a blueprint for your present and nominate a destiny for your future. With that said, one would think you would thoroughly study the procedure of making wise decisions, especially pertaining to relationships. Unfortunately, that is furthest from the truth. Not only do you <u>CONTINUOUSLY</u> make bad decisions in relationship after relationship, you allow those mistakes to vertically challenge your growth by doing nothing to rectify them.

How do you break the cycle?

You break it by tapping into the **root of that fear**! You break it by questioning your outlook on relationships. You literally make valued attempts at discovering what's holding you back from being who you're meant to be in a relationship. Now before you say what I know you are about to say, before you jump off the bridge with that famous excuse of me not understanding how much hurt is attached to your relationship past, let me tell you something!

I'm literally going to give the same reply that was given in my first book "For Her Eyes Only" which is: Blah, Blah, Blah, Blah, Blah, Blah…I'm not trying to be an A hole here, but you need to comprehend that you're not the only one with hurt attached to their past relationship experiences. So get over it! Just let it go! If you seriously want a fresh start at creating an individual worthy of a life partner, there are steps that need to be taken. There is work to be done. There is a guide that you can read.

In my humble opinion, I believe you have selected that correct guide to read. I think you have done a great job with choosing the right material to use as a prep area for creating that relationship masterpiece you desire. "Don't Be An A.S.S All Your Life" is a publication designed to serve as a relationship guide that helps you become a new you by exposing the ASS mentality that unconsciously resides within the present you. Its primary aim is geared toward helping you succeed in your relationship. Its goal is to pull the wool off your eyes so that you can create and execute a plan of action that helps you create a healthy relationship. My way of fulfilling everything that was just promised to you is through personal transparency.

If what you just read so far doesn't entice you to read on, then clearly you love being lost. Oops, I mean, this book is clearly not going to be a help to you. But if you're someone seeking insight on how to possibly improve your relationship experiences, then this is the book for you. If you're someone looking to challenge yourself through viewing personal mistakes, then this is the book for you. Last, if you're someone that is tired of being stuck in the same cycle of relationship mess, then this is the book for you.

Welcome!

INTRODUCTION

Right now, congratulations are in order. This page might say Introduction on it, but in actuality it's the first page of a new relationship life for you. I am so excited! I am so happy for you! I am glad you're open to uncovering the unconscious mistakes made in your relationship. Hooray! Hooray! Hooray! So, now that all that celebratory mushy talk is out of the way, it's time to get into the real purpose behind why you picked up this book.

First and foremost, let me explain the definition of an **ASS** when it comes to relationships. The last thing I would want you thinking is I'm just calling you an ASS just to call you one. The word **ASS** is actually an acronym! An ASS is a person that **Always Surrender Self**, which is what most of you do in relationship after relationship without cognizance. You find yourselves **Always Surrendering Self** to poor communication within your relationships, insecurities of all kind, your own arrogance, as well as your own ignorance. This **ASS** mentality is what has one half of you thinking single-mindedly in relationships and the other half of you not knowing what the hell you're doing in a relationship. These are just plain facts, people! But, the million-dollar question is why are these plain facts?

I believe it's safe to say, we've all made the mistake once or twice of making **"simple things difficult"** and **"difficult things appear simple."** The key phrase I want your focus on for the moment is **"we make difficult things appear simple."** In my opinion, one of the leading problems in a relationship is our attempt at **making difficult things appear simple**. Why do you say that Shaun? It gives this misconception that simplicity is somehow involved with building and sustaining a relationship with someone.

But, here is your NEWS FLASH! There is nothing simple about building a relationship with someone. It's nothing easy about tearing down brick by brick the wall of relationship hang-ups and past failures you have built around your heart to protect it. There is no way a process like this can be simple. So, why do you attempt at making it look simple? I say, "To save face!" I say, "You're scared to ask for relationship help you need!"

I think you realize that asking for help will expose the real problem in your relationship. And your one main **fear** is that YOU ARE THE REAL PROBLEM! You are the root that needs to be addressed. But lucky for you, I have a solution for your concern. One way for you to get over that **<u>fear of exposure</u>** is by posing questions to yourself about yourself and following those questions with honest answers to see what you really need to see.

However, I'm not going to hold my breath with hopes that you follow that advice. Instead you will probably continue to do what you always do, which is conform into a person that Always Surrender Self to everything outside what it takes to sustain a relationship. You will just continue to let past mistakes, society, people, and most important yourselves stand in the way of becoming what you want to be in your relationship. Sad part is most of you really want to believe in relationships! Most of you really want to believe in love, but for some reason you refuse to put in the work it takes to attain it.

That's where I come into the fold. Hopefully, I can rescue you before it's too late. My plan is to introduce you to you, but through me. What did you just say

Shaun? I said my plan is to introduce you to you, but through me. Meaning, I'm going to be transparent with uncovering all the unconscious mistakes made in my past relationships with hopes that it resonates something in you to uncover your mistakes.

I plan to provide you clear insight as to how and why you unconsciously signed on the dotted line of becoming an **ASS** in the first place. I plan on challenging you! I plan on you pushing you to question yourselves on some serious issues. I plan on elevating you to a level of really discovering what's stopping you from enjoying your desired relationship life. However, before we get to work, you need ask yourself some questions. You honestly need to know the stance of your present relationship.

Answer these question for me: what is the position of your relationship right now? Is your relationship stagnant? Is it growing at a rate you desire? You should never be afraid to question the basis of your relationship! What drives it? What formed it? Is it suffering from anything you're doing or have done? For those considering new relationships, these questions should be asked with your past relationships in mind so that you will not make the mistake of bringing past mess into your future bliss.

So while you're contemplating and I hope seriously contemplating, do me a favor! Take this book as an invitation to help you answer those questions. In fact, consider this book a courtesy wake up call. The price you paid for your copy will be 4x as cheap as what you will pay if you continue down your current relationship path. TRUST ME!

With that said, just place your mind on autopilot! I want you to relax! The forecast is projected to start dark and cloudy, but I can guarantee it will end with sunshine if you really take heed to the words that you read in between the pages of this book.

Warning: What you read between the pages of this book might piss you off! But, don't get too frustrated and put the book down. People have always told me that it is better to be pissed off than pissed on. Besides, if I do piss you off, it only means my job is being performed correctly. It just means I have struck a cord that obviously needs to be checked for shortages. It simply means I'm stretching you to fit into new arenas of relationship life. It is all good!

Once the dust settles, you will know that I'm here for you and not against you. You will know that all I want is to help you! You will know that all I want is to better you. You will know that all I want is for you to love being in relationships free of an ASS mentality. All you have to do is just let me prove it!

Turn the page!

THE INVITATION

Shaun, is there something I can do to prevent from Always Surrendering Self?

The answer is yes!

The first thing you must do to prevent from being an **ASS** any longer is acknowledge, accept, and associate what I'm about to reveal to you in this section as the core reasons for your relationship downfalls. Besides that, you can prevent from <u>Always Surrendering Self</u> by simply learning firsthand from a former **ASS** of what not to do in relationships. Welcome to the beginning of Shaun Upshaw's transparency ladies and gentleman! Read and learn!

Out of all the years of being involved in relationships, the one thing I found to be interesting about people is you always seem to find ways of inviting unwanted guests into your relationships. Do you have any clue of what I'm talking about right now? In case you're not aware, there are these pesky guest that you just love to use as a crutch to define the reason for your relationship mentality. Let me tell you what I'm talking about it! The first unwanted guest you invite into your relationships is "Past Relationship Experiences." The second invited unwanted guest you invite is "Friends, also know as Advisors." The third invited unwanted guest you invite into your relationships is what I refer to as "Window-Shopping Relationships." Last, but certainly not least, the biggest unwanted guest you invite is "Roots of family."

These unwanted relationship guests that you love to invite into your relationship home is what strips and tears it apart. I usually don't go out on the limb to generalize everybody, but in this instance, I'm just going to be out there. I believe EVERYBODY has invited at least one, if not all, of the above guests simultaneously into his or her relationship. Anybody that says different, just walk away because you don't need to add a lying spirit to your repertoire of **ASS** behavior.

What you need is someone to keep it real with you. What you need is someone that will put on blast these unwanted relationship guests and the characteristics associated with them. What you need is someone transparent enough to inform you of how these unwanted guests taint your communication, give you ridiculous entitlements, and cloud your relationship mentality. Lucky for you, I am that someone and this book talks about everything you need to be informed of to sustain a healthy relationship. But first things first, let's breakdown these unwanted guest, shall we?

GUEST #1-PAST RELATIONSHIP EXPERIENCES
It is absolutely impossible to move forward with a new relationship when you're always running backwards in everything you say and do. The momentum will eventually halt you! Physics will not allow you and your partner to travel at identical speeds. You will ultimately transform into dead weight, which by the way is difficult to move. Having stated that, why do you constantly reach back for past hurts when dealing with future relationship opportunities? Let's dive into this a little deeper for my reasons as to why I think you do it.

In my opinion, most relationships are entered into based on "fraudulent acts," for lack of a better term. What makes you say that Shaun? I say that because most women tend to build relationships with men that <u>appear</u> to show stability. And on the other hand, most men get into relationships because a woman has shown some type of loyalty that makes her <u>appear</u> more trust worthy than any other women he has dealt with in his life.

Honestly speaking, neither reason is a real reason to get into a relationship with someone, but hey it happens. Nevertheless, the one word I want your attention focused on right now is <u>appear</u>. My reason for that is simple! Appearance is the one key word that will help you discover the real problem as to why you keep dragging past baggage into future relationships. Check this out. I believe the appearance of a past something in your life is what stands in the way of you facing the reality of future someone for your life.

Wait a minute Shaun, are you somehow implying it's my fault I cannot find the right person? Yes! I am saying it's your fault, but it's not completely your fault. Your fault in this matter comes from your inability to recognize that you select an appearance of someone, rather than take time to face reality of self. Let me explain.

In most cases, you tend to choose relationship partners that seem to have characteristics you believe are missing within you. However, the issue with doing something like that is most of you don't have a clue of who you really are, which leads me with one question. If you're not sure of who you really are then how do you know if people you're choosing really have something you're missing?

That is why I'm calling for an investigation. I'm asking for you to evaluate rather than keep bad experiences in your memory bank. Ask yourselves this question for me. Do you honestly believe that bad past experiences play any kind of a part in sustaining future relationship opportunities? Before you attempt to justify that question with an excuse not a real answer, let me stop you in your tracks by saying no.

The only thing that bad past experiences do is push your future opportunities into suffering. Bad past experiences will not give the 100% of you a future opportunity deserves. Bad past experiences will do nothing more then stand in your way of becoming a person with visible relationship qualities that someone designed to share life with you can see.

Be honest right now! Aren't you tired of jumping from relationship to relationship using your past as a tool for direction? Aren't you tired of hiding all the cracks in your <u>appeared</u> wholeness? Aren't you exhausted from carrying all that unnecessary baggage?

Whether you be honest about it or not, this unwanted guest of past experiences you continuously invite into your relationships is a problem. Moreover, it is a problem that you create for yourself. It is completely asinine to drag your past into new relationships and have enough nerve to expect for it to succeed. I don't know what world you reside in, but it doesn't work that way in the real world.

As I said in the beginning, the first thing you have to do is <u>acknowledge</u> it's happening. Then, move forward by <u>accepting</u> that in some degree past experiences are the common denominator for you not receiving what you desire from relationships. From there, you have to end this nonsense it by never again <u>associating</u> bad past experiences with future relationship opportunities.

At some point, you have to acknowledge, accept, and associate this guest as a relationship nemesis. Now say it with me! I will no longer allow this guest to stand in my way of future opportunities! I will accept the challenge of facing my part of the problem! I Don't Want To Be An ASS All My Life! Let's move on!

GUEST #2-FRIENDS

One aspect of a relationship you often ignore is friends are not supposed to be involved in it. There are a host of reasons why they shouldn't be involved, but for now let me give you two key ones. When offering relationship advice, most of your friends' are bias toward the friendship rather than relationship. In my opinion, their judgment is cloudy. Furthermore, in most cases they are going through the same or worst problems in their relationship. But, let's not forget about the number one reason that leads all reasons by a landslide: <u>**MOST OF YOUR FRIENDS ARE SINGLE**</u> or <u>**IN RELATIONSHIPS WITH A SINGLE PERSON'S MENTALITY!**</u>

Here's some helpful advice! A fast way to attach a single status to your name is by listening to friends who don't have enough vision to see through their own mess, but somehow has enough sense to offer solutions on how to get out of yours. However, an even faster way to find yourself checking the single status box is listening to advice from your single friends. I have two questions for you: (1) How can a friend in an identical circumstance know exactly what advice to give you, but can't seem to comprehend what to give themselves? (2)

What good relationship advice could you possibly gain from friends operating out of a single person's mentality?

If you were to answer those two questions with pure honesty, your eyes will begin to see what I see, which is placing friends in your relationship isn't a smart idea. You also will see that unwanted guest #2 is by far one of the leading causes for friction in relationships. I often find myself amazed at how people continue to solicit advice from friends about (1) a person their friend is not in a relationship with and (2) a person whose character perception is given to them by you. How can a friend give accurate advice standing on one side of the fence?

Having stated that, can you now understand why I say a friend's advice could sway you right into being an ASS? What makes this situation even more unreal is sometimes a friend's advice usually points you in a direction that only benefits you, not help you. Why? In most cases, friends are only giving you what you want to hear instead of what you need to hear because most of these so-called friends won't be bold enough to step on your toes. They're more concerned with sustaining the friendship versus informing you of your mistakes to sustain your relationship.

However, it goes deeper than just that aspect of it. The one vital element you're forgetting when asking for advice from a friend is where their foundation of advice stems from, which is more than likely past experiences. Right now, you should be having the light bulb effect.

Why? We just discussed it! That's why!

Do you recall everything I just said concerning unwanted relationship guest #1? Okay, well let's put it all together so I can show you something remarkable. I need you to really pay attention here because you need to understand clearly what you're about to read. The advice your friends offer sometimes is doing nothing more than adding to the room you're already housing your unwanted relationship guest #1. How?

Your friend's advice is adding to it because your friends are inviting their unwanted guest #1 into the room where you house your unwanted guest #1. Not only is your friend possibly rendering bad advice based on the status of their current relationship experience, but also they're reaching in the archives of past experiences to justify their advice. What hurts you in this situation is if the friend offering advice has not mentally accepted any fault in the downfall of their past or current relationship, then the blind will be definitely leading the blind here.

Now, as far as your single friends' advice goes, the majority of times, their perspective is so filled with bitterness, along with the fact their misery would love your company, it's almost a crime for them to even be offering you advice. In fact, your single friends have mastered what I like to call "entitlement audacity" Yeah, you saw it right! I said "entitlement audacity."

What is entitlement audacity? It's when your single friends all of a sudden begin to feel entitled to give advice concerning your relationship whether it's warranted or not. Your single friends begin to also feel entitled as well comfortable enough to check your mate regarding certain relationship issues you've shared in confidence with them. Before you know it, your partner is now in a relationship with you and your friends.

At the end of the day, we both know where that road leads, which is you joining those pack of entitled single friends, but as a single woman. That's why it is imperative for you to know why unwanted guest #2 is no friend to your relationship, especially if you desire one that will last. I really hope this section is currently expanding your sense of sight right now because unwanted guest #2 will forever be a hindrance to your relationship until you recognize it. More importantly, you will continue to be an **ASS** until this guest is no longer welcomed in your relationship. You better kick friends out of your relationship and keep that door closed!

GUEST #3-WINDOW SHOPPING
RELATIONSHIPS

This unwanted guest has employed more people to be an **ASS** than any corporation I can think of right now. This unwanted guest is with certainty considered a major contributor as to why people **"Always Surrender Self."** I personally have witnessed a mass amount of couples suffer in their relationship because of unwanted guest #3.

The "Window-Shopping Relationship" is best classified as a relationship that looks good from the outside, but once you try on the experience for yourself, it's not at all what you assumed it to be. Everyone, including me, has at least made the mistake of taking a glance at another relationship with hopes of possibly emulating it in your relationship. It's almost human nature to want something you perceive as "A Successful Relationship" for your own.

However, there are a few things to consider when desiring to emulate another couple. The first thing to consider would be, are you willing to experience the same experiences those people you're trying to "copy and paste" into your relationship has experienced? Next thing to consider is do you really know the true character of the people in that relationship you're trying to emulate? Last thing to consider is why choose to live by relationship rules and standards of another couple when you have liberty to create your own?

Let's dive into this discussion a little further. The first question was: Are you willing to experience those same experiences of the people you're trying to "copy and paste" into your relationship has experienced? The answer should be no. Scratch that because the answer should be a HELL NO! What you fail to realize is everyone is designed to experience relationships in a contrasting manner. It is beyond insane to value another person's relationship experience over yours because you actually don't have anything to gain from it.

Now don't get me wrong, you can definitely learn from watching other peoples' relationships. But yearning for an identical relationship is asking for nothing but heartache, headaches, and eventually the feeling to eradicate the very thoughts of entertaining a relationship all together. In a nutshell, here is what transpires once you decide to place another relationship on a pedestal above your own.

It becomes heartache because once your relationship never aligns with the relationship you're trying to emulate, your feelings become hurt. Then, arguments ensue because that's usually the action that follows hurt feelings. From there, arguments transform into headaches because you're steadily trying to discover why your mate is so opposed to becoming a carbon copy of a relationship you deem as successful. Then finally, all roads lead to the inevitable. You put an end to the very thought of entertaining relationships all together because heartache gave you an illusion of failure. Whereas your headaches from attempting to force your mate to become someone other than themselves, frustrated you to a point of no return.

Then what?

The relationship will fail miserably because your partner refused to follow the blueprint of a relationship you deemed as successful. That is the then what! Let's continue!

The next thing I warned you to consider pertaining to "Window-Shopping Relationships" is do you really know the true character of the people in the relationship you're trying to emulate? One thing I know about people in these "Window-Shopping Relationships" is their character tends to be a little questionable. They're usually one way in the sunlight and another way by dark fall.

These people have managed to become so good at pretending for an audience, they sometimes forget their true identity once the curtains close. Somehow you start to think this type of couple can walk on water, but in reality their relationship is very titanic-like, which means it's sinking slowly.

After reading that I know the question in your mind right now. You are asking me, why do I fall for those shenanigans? Great question! You fall for such nonsense and shenanigans because you're in love with the idea that a relationship can be perfect. You love the feeling of Always Surrendering Self to what looks good! You just love being an ASS when it comes to situations like this ladies and gentleman! It just feels so damn good! Jokes aside, what you're doing is totally misplacing your common sense with the belief that these fictitious "Window-Shopping Relationships" have perfection associated with them.

Fundamentally, what you're doing is permitting people's depiction of what a relationship should be to overrule what your relationship has to be for it to gain sustaining success. This is why you have to be very careful what you allow your eyes to emulate. You must come to grips with understanding that everything is not what it appears to be. Not only that, but here's a little something extra that will shine a light on these "Window Shopping Relationships."

In the majority of these cases, the two people you so desperately want to emulate for your relationship, can't even break up if they wanted to. Why? It would tarnish the image of bull$h!t they've been feeding you to make it seem as if perfection is capable of existing in relationships. That's Why! The one thing to consider regarding these relationships is usually people who are in them focus more on keeping the watchful eye of people satisfied rather than being transparent about the imperfections in their relationship. What it comes down to is you have to make careful decisions on what relationship ideology you invite into your relationship, which segues into my final point.

The last thing I asked you to consider before praising "Window Shopping Relationships" is: Why choose to live by relationship rules and standards of another couple when you have liberty to create your own? This consideration doesn't warrant a long drawn out explanation because it's very simple to explain. In fact, I will extend the courtesy of putting every word in large bold caps and separating it from the rest of the text so that you can see and understand clearly. Here we go!

PEOPLE, YOU THE HAVE FREEDOM TO MAKE YOUR OWN RELATIONSHIP RULES AND STANDARDS.

I often find myself wondering if you really know that piece of information about your relationship. I discussed in the beginning of this section, you've become an ASS by conforming. Well here is your opportunity to resist conforming. Please recognize that you have options and those options don't have to be centered on anybody else's relationship except your own. Real talk!

Once you form a relationship with someone, in essence, you and that person have entered a personal contract. The two of you decide the terms, expectations, and violations of that contract. Nothing in that contract should be contingent upon what others say or appear to be. The overall terms of your contract should establish you and your partner's mutual happiness. The expectations should delegate accountability amongst each other. Lastly, the violations should inform your significant other of what will transpire if the terms of your relationship is violated. Your violations shouldn't match anybody else's relationship violations. Point, blank, and period!

And to put the icing on the cake, this entire process shouldn't involve past interactions, chatter from friends, or mirages of what you think are perfect relationships. The establishment of your relationship rules and standards is a responsibility solely given to you and your mate. It doesn't get much simpler than that, my friends.

Guess my main point is the assumption of "what's good for the goose is good for the gander" needs to cease. For you to assume that because something looks good in one relationship that it will look good in yours is ridiculous. You have to remember the window-shopping displays that have mannequins in them are strategically placed there to get your attention. Those displays are purposed to get you in the store to buy something; mainly, something you can't afford in the first place. So, you need to start counting the cost, ladies and gentleman.

Next time you see something that looks good, before you consider investing in it, ask yourselves one question: **Is the price worth the title of being an ASS all your life?**

GUEST #4- ROOTS OF FAMILY

I am not ashamed to admit that unwanted relationship guest #4 ended just about all of my relationships. In fact, I'm willing to bet this guest is probably ruining most of your relationships as well. Out of the entire invited unwanted relationship guest list that keeps you an ASS, this guest is #1 and holds the lead by a very large margin. Nothing and I do mean nothing ruins a relationship faster than the "Roots Of Family."

The best way to describe the detriment this unwanted guest causes is by using myself as an example first. I can do that because this guest was the main guest that visited my relationships. I have first hand experience with this one people. Lets talk about it!

My father was a man that seemed to keep a variety of female companions with no commitment to any of them. My mother on the other hand was overly committed in her relationships even if those relationships were failing miserably. Although both experiences were of opposite extremes, I learned some valuable information from both. As I carefully watched their relationships, I knew then my relationships had to be different. Or so I thought!

Now, I'm going to stop right there to pose a question. I want you to be honest with yourselves about this question. The question is how many of you have vowed not to repeat your parents' relationship footsteps? While you take time to hopefully be honest with that question, I'm going to simultaneously let you in on a secret and pick up the tail end of my story.

In my efforts of trying so hard not to be my parents in relationships, I actually became them unconsciously. Let me explain! Not only in some of my relationships did I lack commitment through selfishness, but I also found myself staying in some relationships that were long overdue for a break up. The very two elements I vowed not to allow in my relationships became the identical elements that eventually hurt my relationships.

The characteristics of both my parents unconsciously damaged me. I say that with confidence because I often found myself expending too much energy either being selfish by lacking commitment or being weak by staying in toxic relationships. Right now you're probably thinking that I'm pointing the finger at my parents for my shortcomings, but that's not the case. What I'm actually doing is highlighting a character flaw many people unconsciously obtain from parents, family, or guardians by observing their relationships while growing up. That is what makes this unwanted guest so dangerous. In a sense, this guest invites itself to you, but you leave the door open for it to be a squatter in your world by not acknowledging, accepting, and associating it as poisonous to your relationship.

There is saying that goes "Mirror, Mirror on the wall. Guess I'm my parents after all." The bottom line of that saying is, whether it's your mother or father, inevitably, one of your parents' traits will rub off on you. In my case, I just was cursed with both traits, which is why I'm in the position to warn you of this nonsense. The roots of family have the capabilities to strangle the life out of every relationship you find yourselves in. If you don't believe me, you should know by now that I am more than willing to provide an example to prove my point.

Example:

Say, a young lady grows up in a single parent household where she hears nothing but negativity spewed from her mother's mouth about men and relationships. To further detail this illustration, let's say this young lady has a huge amount of aunts' and older cousins that validate her mother's every word. What do you think is going to eventually happen to that young lady? Let me do the honor of informing you!

As time passes she will begin to authorize all that negativity to take lead in her mind. Even if she does discover success in a relationship, those negative roots that were planted, nourished, and cared for by those people surrounding her growing up will overrule the success. Here's why! No matter the possibilities of success in a relationship, if she hasn't completely uprooted everything she has negatively heard regarding relationships before entering into hers, then more than likely her relationship is bound to fail.

It will fail because whenever her mate doesn't live up to her given expectation, then those negative roots planted within her growing up will begin to resonate negativity. For example, let's say her mother's biggest planted root was telling her daughter to never trust men. If that's the case, any failed expectations will remind her of why she should not trust men. I'm not trying to give you any corner store psychology. I'm merely telling you what is real. While you attempt to prove me wrong, I'm moving on because all this goes deeper than what you're reading right now.

Truth of the matter is I could go on for days with example after example of how roots of family can flag your relationships with failure. But it wouldn't matter, especially if you're not in position to acknowledge, accept, and associate it as a cause for relationship faults. I would literally be wasting time, ink, and paper. So, instead of wasting valuable time, I would rather spend my time doing something more productive such as what I'm about to do with the remaining of these pages.

The Wrap-Up

Clearly, you have been bombarded with a lot of information to reflect on in this first section. However, this is merely the beginning people. As previously stated, it goes deeper than just telling you about theses unwanted guest you invite into your relationship. You have to call on some relationship memories and self-realness to see where you stand in this situation. All I did here was provide a menu of options you never thought to consider because you were too busy ordering up the same nonsense to believe each time you came across a problem of a failing relationship. I simply wanted to give you a peak into what you been unconsciously inviting into your relationship. It doesn't look so appetizing now, does it?

But, on a serious note, if you wholeheartedly want to stop acting as an ASS, the next few sections on the characteristics attached to these unwanted guests should closely be paid attention to. This is where I give you my mistakes on a platter and go deep into how these characteristics are triggered from your invited unwanted guests.

Anytime you feel any of what you're reading doesn't directly apply to you, I ask that you don't disregard the information. I actually beg you to just open your mind up because I know you will find your mess hiding somewhere in between these pages.

All right! Here we go! The time is here! It is about to get real!

Turn the page!

TAINTED COMMUNICATION FORMULA

Remember when I said your invited unwanted guest have bad characteristics attached to them, well here is the first of three characteristics that come along with that invitation.

What is a tainted communication formula?

It is communication that has more than likely become your unconscious way of communicating in your relationship. I know you're probably saying, "What in the hell are you talking about, Shaun?" But trust me on this one. It will begin to make sense by the end of this section. I promise! Just hear me out!

The tainted communication formula is a characteristic that derives from whichever unwanted guests you most invite into your relationships. To explain this more clearly, I'm going to use me as an example. From guest #1 to guest #4, every unwanted guest I ever invited into my relationships left me with a tainted form of communication. It basically provided me some immature tactics that eventually transformed into my tainted communication formula.

I did not discover this bit of information about my tainted communicating until I stopped pointing the finger of blame at my partners for the communication failures in my relationships. I basically forced myself to be real with myself. And you have to do the same if you really want to gain the real on how you communicate in your relationships. But anyway, after keeping it real with myself, my tainted communication formulas became so evident that I had to seriously evaluate the origin of them.

Here I was at one point thinking: Shaun D. Upshaw is a prime catch when it comes to communicating. But, in reality, my communication had managed to become tainted due to my unconscious relationship hang-ups. Truth be told, there are plenty of you that suffer from this same affliction, but you just will not be real about it. What's stopping me from admitting it then Shaun?

Well reader, how many people do you know willing to admit something is wrong with them? One thing I discovered about people is you truly love to be in position to communicate what the next person's contribution to a failed or failing relationship is, rather than speak one sentence about your wrongdoings. And that mistake alone is what makes you an ASS ladies and gentleman. The fact that you cannot honestly admit your portion as to why communication failed or is currently failing in your relationship produces a person that Always Surrender Self. It just so happens, that you're waving the white flag of surrender to your own bull$h*t.

I understand that might come off as a tad bit harsh, but in my opinion, harsh truth is what gets your attention. At the end of the day, the time has come for you to put your big boy/girl underwear on and just evaluate your communication formula, especially if you find that communication in your relationship is more hostile than peaceful. It is time to discover if your way of communicating is tainted or not. The reason is being privy to such information is the determining factor of whether your relationship fails or sustain.

So, what I'm about to do for you right now is explain the three communication tactics that made up my communication formula. I will forewarn that some of you might be able to identify with my tactics whereas some of you might not. However, I guarantee once you read about mine, it will trigger which tactics you do use in your communication. As always, all I ask is that you keep an open mind, open heart, and transparent mentality to accept whatever you get from the reading. Let's get started!

COMMUNICATION TACTICS

How you communicate in your relationship will determine the success or failure of it. But you should already know that much, right? So let's jump to the real issue, which is: why do you find yourselves more on the failing rather than successful end of communicating in relationships. I could provide you multiple answers as to why, but for the sake of time let's address the core of this issue.

In my honest opinion, the core issue is you just don't want to leave your *"communication comfort zone."* Plain and simple! You sincerely believe your way of communicating is just fine. After all, it has successfully gotten you into plenty of relationships. However, on the flip side, your way of communicating has also gotten you involved in plenty of break ups as well. Guaranteed! But, it's up to you to admit that reality.

One of the biggest problems you usually suffer from with communication in your relationship is being blinded with naïve ignorance to think your style of communication shouldn't be altered in any way. You tend to feel your partner should just get on your page and compromise his/her communication style to fit your style. Sounds fair, right? Well, not only is that not fair, but it's wrong on many levels. I told you earlier about how you seem to like waving the white flag of surrender to your own nonsense, didn't I? It's nothing but ASS behavior at its finest.

But in case you forgot what I said about it, here you go. Being an ASS to your own BS is a terrible space to be in, especially being involved in a relationship. Why? Simple. You and your logics become unreasonable in your communication! You don't see anything past what you're saying. And compromising is thrown completely out the window.

Trust me, I know the type. I once was the type. I once was a person that cared more about being an ASS than a person who cared about his relationship sustaining. That alone should qualify a listening ear on this subject matter. Right?

As I glance back on my past relationships, I'm ashamed of the way some of them ended. But in the same breath, I'm glad my relationships ended that way. If it were not for communication breakdowns and constant failure in my relationships, I wouldn't be in a position to tell you how being an ASS will have you single or stagnant in your relationships. I wouldn't be able to speak on these ridiculous tactics that made up my communication formula. In fact, let's just jump right into these old communication tactics of mine.

The first communication tactic I used in my past relationships was "**Assumptions vs. Speculations.**" The second communication tactic was entitled "**Get Over it.**" The last communication tactic was called "**Bait.**" Basically, what it boils down to is instead of communicating in a way that would've sustained some of my past relationships, I allowed these tactics to concoct a tainted communicate formula for me to use in my relationships. Real talk, people! Pay attention!

TACTIC #1-ASSUMPTIONS VS. SPECULATIONS
Although many would consider, "Assumptions and Speculations" to be similar, they actually are used in different manners within relationships. Assumptions are

something you believe to be true, but lack necessary evidence to support your belief whereas speculation is guessing, but leaving the possibility for other options to be heard.

That is primarily the difference in a nutshell. The question now become after reading the definition of "Assumptions vs. Speculations", which side of the fence are you playing the most when communicating in your relationship? Be honest. I will even give you a moment to look around and see if anybody is near you. I know how you feel about admitting relationship faults when people are around to witness it. You know what, my bad! Excuse my sarcasm; I could not help myself. Every moment I get to point out ASS behavior, I jump at it. Nonetheless, let's get back on the subject.

What is an example of an assumption you used to communicate in your past relationships Shaun?

Great question! An assumption I often used in my relationships was assuming that my partner was having sex with her friends of the opposite sex. There was never any real proof to support my assumption, but "who the hell needed it" was my mindset. During that time, making assumptions was the main way I communicated to my partner. I know you are more then likely over there wondering what was I actually attempting to communicate with that terrible tactic, but don't worry I'm about to tell you.

I basically used this tactic to validate my indiscretions. I assumed my mate was sleeping with her male friends because I was actually sleeping with most of my female friends. Therefore, to make me feel better about my unfaithful actions, it was only right in my eyes to validate myself by covering up my BS and placing my wrongs on my partner. I don't know if you've picked up on this by now, but guest #4 clearly is running all up and through here. Don't believe me just go back to first section and read about how guest # 4 affected me. I mean here's pure honesty at its finest along with a example of what an ASS looks like.

The question now is, how many of you are willing to step up to the honesty plate and take a swing at figuring out why you do it? Any takers? Don't be shy? I know most of you at some point have used assumptions as a way to cover something up. How many of you are willing to lay it out on the table and explain your reason behind using it? While you figure that out, let's move on to speculation because I think you're getting the picture now.

SPECULATIONS

The main distinction between speculating and assuming is at least with speculation you're smart enough to leave room for it to be proven false. But in my opinion, speculation is just as bad. It's the gateway behavior that leads to assumptions. I honestly believe too much speculating will eventually transform you into an assumer. Believe me, I know all about it! That's why I'm alarming you of the dangers this part of the tactic can be in your communication and why you shouldn't do it.

Let's go into this more deeply for you to better understand! The main reason I speculated in most relationships was because of my bad experiences from my past relationships. Instead of letting those particular bad experiences stay in those particular past relationships, it made perfect sense to just speculate that the same will happen in every relationship moving forward. (Refer back to unwanted guest #1 if want to refresh your memory)

What it ultimately comes down to is I was trying to hide my insecurities. I had confidence issues during those times. I wasn't completely stable in who Shaun was as a person, which made me not secure of who Shaun was to whatever person I was in a relationship with. My incapability to communicate that insecurity ultimately turned out to be the overall basis for using speculation in my relationships. Do you see now how it became so easy for me to move from speculating to assuming and from assuming to ALWAYS SURRENDING SELF? My unwillingness to let go of (Unwanted Guest #1) caused me to fall into (Unwanted Guest #4) more easily, which in turn made me an ASS because I didn't want admit to none of it.

DRAWN CONCLUSION

At the end of the day, both my assumptions and speculations stemmed from 2 guests I invited into my relationship. Instead of being upfront and communicating with my partner about my past experiences, or better yet letting go of it, I allowed it to graduate into validating myself as to why I shouldn't remain faithful. In the end, I cheated myself out of relationship success with many good women. I manipulated myself into believing this communication tactic protected me, when all it did was hinder me.

If you're a person that assumes and speculates in your relationship, then you need to stop doing it. More significantly, you need to face the unwanted guest or guests that contributes to you using this tactic to communicate in your relationships. This particular communication tactic doesn't add anything positive to any formula that leads to a successful relationship. All it does is lead to a dead end road. Furthermore, it keeps you an ASS all your life, especially if you continue to decline the opportunity to fix the real problem, which is you.

TACTIC #2 –GET OVER IT

Whenever I think about this communication tactic, one word comes to mind. That one word is **SELFISHNESS.** The "Get Over It" communication tactic, without a doubt, is the biggest contributor to communication failures in relationships. Basically, this tactic is what ruined all phases of communication in just about all of my relationships. This tactic definitely has that ability!

The "Get Over It" tactic is just what it sounds like when you read it. It is you unconsciously communicating to your partner via words or actions to get over whatever feelings they're feeling about something because it's not important enough to address. Outside of the obvious, what makes this tactic deadly is at some point in the relationship you begin to totally disregard your partner's feelings altogether. You ultimately force your partner to either (A) suppress their feelings or (B) find someone else to communicate whatever they were attempting to communicate with you.

These options in no way are beneficial to a relationship. For example, if your partner chooses option (A), then you run the risk of your mate blowing up on you. He or she will literally snap off one day without warning because that's exactly what happens when a person continuously suppress with no option to release. Also, they begin to record all that suppression into their memory bank as a bad relationship experience. (Remember Guest #1) Now, if your partner chooses option (B), then you basically just invited cheating into your relationship, or even worse, the advice of friends. (Refer to guest #2 if you forgot the detriment of that happening)

Nevertheless, my reason for using this "Get Over It" tactic was I didn't want our relationship focused on anything outside of me. I didn't care to communicate about anything that didn't involve me. I know that sounds like an insane way to communicate in a relationship, but I did warn you this specific tactic is centered on selfishness. And before you release your judgment, I need you to know there are masses of you right now unconsciously communicating this way in your relationship. So place that judgment back in the holster because you're not as innocent as you think ladies and gentleman.

> **Side Bar:** I don't know if you've picked up on this or not while reading, but this communication tactic has capabilities of producing two ASSES out of the situation. Of course, one ASS is the person that convinces him/her self that selfishness is a valuable asset to have in a relationship. However, the other ASS in this equation is the person who becomes manipulated into allowing selfish behavior to roam free in that relationship. I guess you thought those people were getting a pass in the matter. Wrong! Both parties, with certainty, are surrendering self, but just in different capacities.

> One is an ASS for obvious reasons whereas the other is an ASS for allowing that way of

communicating to go on in the relationship. Honestly speaking, both of them need to do some self-evaluating because both are suffering from the effects of an unwanted guest. Or am I just the only one over here seeing the revelation unfold?

Nonetheless, bottom line is a relationship should not be susceptible to entertaining this communication tactic because it holds no future. Selfishness doesn't breed success in any relationship. Nor does accepting selfishness. All you have is one person lying down while the other walks all over them. After carefully evaluating why I used this tactic to communicate, I realized that my roots of family had deep hooks in me. I also had something else attached to me that cause me to act that way, which will be discussed in the next attached characteristic section.

But ultimately, what I did was allow my father's selfishness in relationships to unconsciously latch on to me. (Unwanted guest #4) Instead of learning how to properly communicate with whomever I was with at that time, I chose selfishness as my way to communicate in the relationship. Instead of understanding communication is a two way street, I turned into a one way with no outlet. I unconsciously surrendered myself to my communication paradigm witnessed while growing up.

DRAWN CONCLUSION

The fact that I unconsciously committed such ignorant communication tactics in my past relationships really baffles me. And in the midst of this amazement, it leads me to warn you how dangerous it is for you to be wrapped up in your own selfishness and nonsense. If you have selected to use this "Get Over It" tactic as a part of your communication, you better get prepared for a lifetime of singleness.

Not only that, you will continue to be an ASS until this tactic is evaluated to comprehend your real motivation for using it. As I been stating all along, you just have to be real with yourself during this process in order to properly dissolve it. So while you make the decision as to what to do, I have a question to leave in your spirit. How long will you allow this "Get Over It" tactic to stand in the way of properly communicating in your relationship? Let's move on!

TACTIC #3- BAIT

Bait is a communication tactic most if not all people have used before in a relationship. One main reason people use this tactic is because they are usually fishing for a specific response about something pertaining to the relationship. Instead of just coming right out with whatever they desire to know, he/she finds it more beneficial to be elusive rather than direct.

The one factor that makes this tactic deadly is eventually you will begin to communicate in code. Code is a way of communicating that hides rather than put in plain sight what you really want to know from your partner. I used bait in my relationships because talking in code about certain subjects felt better than talking direct. Why? Two reasons! (1) I wanted to stay away from possibly hurting my partner's feelings concerning certain subjects. (2) I feared my partner would look at me in a different manner if I expressed interest in something that many would consider crazy.

The overall main reason goes by the name of **unwanted guest #3,** which is **window-shopping relationship.** This guest definitely had a hand in planting a false sense of what I needed for my relationship to be successful. Let me explain.

Transparency Moment: One of my ex girlfriends and I were double dating with another couple. We were having some interesting dialogue about sex in relationships. We somehow got on the conversation of how much sex is too much sex in a relationship. The young lady on the opposite side of the table responded by saying, "There is no such thing as too much sex." She then followed that response by saying, "I give it to my man anytime he wants it."

Immediately, my brain went into a wow moment. To know a woman existed that believed in giving sex to her man anytime he wanted it was music to my ears. The only bad thing about hearing such great music was at that time I was in a relationship with a person that didn't tune into that channel. So what do you think happened next?

Instead of having an open and real conversation with that particular girlfriend about my desire to up the ante in the sex department, I used the "Bait" tactic to communicate and get my answers. Now, there are two ways to bait people. You can do it in a positive or negative way. This particular time I selected the positive bait.

> **Side Bar:** The reason I used positive bait for this particular situation is because I knew negative bait wouldn't get her to open up as much to the conversation. Nine out of ten times, negative bait would have caused a problem to arise. Why? It's because negative bait can come off as comparing your partner whereas positive bait is disarming your partner. For this particular situation, I needed her to be disarmed instead of feeling compared to another woman and how she pleases her man.

So, the first thing I did on the car ride home that night was bait her by appearing shocked and appalled by this young lady's willingness to give sex to her man anytime he wanted it. Then I further baited her by asking what she felt about the young lady's response.

To make a long story short, I completely wasted my time with my indirect inquires. To top it off, I didn't even achieve hearing my desired response. She actually had taken my indirect approach as a sign of disgust with the situation.

It didn't prompt her to change not one view on the amount of sex she was giving up, but that's not even the crazy part. What happened from that point moving forward is a prime example of why using "Bait" as a communication tactic made me an ASS. My relationship eventually failed because my assumed need for our relationship to be successful was never met. I basically ended that relationship by surrendering to the appeared success of another relationship.

This tactic basically caused me to lose a great woman by baiting her instead of being upfront and accepting her response whether I agreed with it or not. What I did was put that woman in an unsuccessful situation.

By her not answering in a way I didn't wanted to hear, it left me unsatisfied; therefore, placing an unnecessary rift and void that didn't exist prior to me falling for the appeared success of another couple's sexual relationship.

The crux of what I'm saying is this "Bait" tactic is a remedy for communication failure. It reeks of nothing but game playing, and the last timed checked, game playing shouldn't be a part of any relationship. In essence what I did was trade in a good woman that supplied my actual needs for an illusion of a woman that planted in my mind an assumed need. I thought the grass was greener on the other side, but I failed to look for the weeds hiding in between the blades of greenness.

Now, I know you might not have used bait in the identical manner I used it. But, I know you use it. And I know you use it to fish for specific answers about something you refuse to be direct about with your partner. You don't have to lie about it.

The truth is everyone uses "Bait" until they come to grips with who they are and what they really desire from their relationship. It's just a game of manipulation that is unavoidable. Everyone in some way has manipulated his/her partner at some point. If you say anything opposite, not only are you a liar, but you also are a person that is manipulating yourself at this very moment. So stop it!

THE WRAP UP
So there you have it ladies and gentleman, the communication tactics that tainted my communication formula. If you were paying closing attention, you would've grasp that personal nonsense, insecurity,

selfishness, confusion, and game playing combined with all 4 unwanted guests is what made up my communication formula in my relationships. You also would've picked up on what makes up your communication formula if you were honest with yourselves about it.

What it boils down to is: a tainted communication formula is merely the icebreaker of what comes along with these unwanted guests you invite into your relationships. This characteristic is the least of your worries. There are two other bad characteristics left to discuss that makes this one look like a walk in the park.

But don't worry about it. I was here to break down this tainted communication formula, so I will be here to do the same for the rest. I just hope you're getting a glimpse at the seriousness behind inviting these unwanted guests into your relationships. If you haven't seen it yet, you better brace yourselves because it goes deeper and gets even more ugly.

Turn the page at your own risk!

UNWRITTEN ENTITLEMENTS

After reading about that tainted communication formula, you probably over there saying, "Can it get any worse?" The answer is yes! Besides a tainted communication formula, another bad characteristic these invited unwanted guest bring into your relationship is "Unwritten Entitlements." Now, I understand there are certain things in relationships you are rightfully entitled to such as faithfulness, respect, and consideration just to name a few. But, I'm referring to those unconscious entitlements that are placed on your relationship partner that is not their void to fill.

I don't care what person you hire to dress it up! I don't care what person you summon to justify it! There is absolutely no convincing me that these particular entitlements I'm talking about are the responsibility of your partner to pacify. The general point I'm attempting to drive home here is: it's not the job of your relationship partner to deal with these specific entitlements because the job belongs to you, and only you, especially since these entitlements are brought into the relationship by you and forced upon your partner to deal with. Allow me to explain more in detail!

INSECURITY VALIDATION

The most common found "Unwritten Entitlement" in a relationship is *insecurity validation.* Whenever someone inquires about some of my downturns in past relationships, I always seem to spotlight *insecurity validation* as one of the leading causes for why my past relationships stayed in turmoil. In fact, it's probably why some of your relationships are in turmoil as well. Shaun, would you mind telling me what is *insecurity validation?*

Sure! It is an entitlement where you believe your mate is responsible for validating your insecurities. Honestly, it's nothing more than a crutch you continuously use to keep excuses in arms reach. What excuses? The excuses as to why you cannot be the desired partner you're called to be in your relationship. In a nutshell, this entitlement is a problem and a huge one.

One of the things that make *insecurity validation* a huge problem is, in most cases, you don't even recognize you're doing it. This *insecurity validation* is one of the central reasons your relationship path stays on a collision course with failure. Guess why? Your inability to let go of inviting these unwanted guests in to your relationship is why! Nonsense like this is what keeps failure looming around your relationships. And it is definitely worth paying some attention to!

So, while I explain more about *insecurity validation,* as well as the other unwritten entitlements in this section, I request that you dig deep within self to discover the origin of your unwritten entitlements. Before you say, 'Shaun, I don't have any unwritten entitlements," just know I will be helping you with the digging. I'm willing to expose my unwritten entitlements along with why I used them in order to help you through this process. Although I'm certain our entitlements will not share the same origin, I believe you can discover yours in the midst of me telling you about mine.

For those of you not prepared to dig deep, then it's a safe say you have met your stopping destination in this book. However, if curiosity to discover something about yourself, the will to do better, and the attitude to no longer accept failure in your relationship drives you, then please continue. I thank you in advance for attempting to go through the process! Now let's get into talking more about this *insecurity validation*! Listen up!

I think a great job has been done of consistently stating to this point that whatever unwanted guest you unconsciously invite into your relationships, is the exact guest that mainly contributes to your downfall. The same applies here! Whatever unwanted guest you unconsciously invite into your relationship is the exact guest that helps you draft your unwritten entitlements.

> **Transparency Moment:** There is no better way to explain *insecurity validation* then to just tell you where this entitlement derived in me and how it affected my past relationships.

> One of my biggest insecurities in past relationships was the need to be **reassured** that my lady would be there for me no matter the circumstance. The most transparent way to describe why I needed that reassurance is guest #4, which is the root of family.

> Let's just say, I had a hard time with uprooting the dysfunction my family planted within me

regarding relationships. Now, I want you to pay close attention here because I don't want you to miss this!

Do you remember me saying in the beginning that unfortunately both of my parents' relationship traits rubbed off on me? Well, those traits of lacking commitment and staying in toxic relationships were the identical traits that not only tainted my communication, but it also gave me insecurities.

How did that happen? Superb question! It happened because during that time, my parents' traits were the only examples I had to define a relationship. In my world, relationships had to either experience broken promises & selfishness and/or inability to leave despite toxicity for it to work.

The reason I didn't have a problem with believing such nonsense was, as I said before, I saw women stay with my father in spite of his broken promises & selfishness and witnessed my mother stay in her relationships in spite of evident proof for a breakup. Ultimately, experiencing such ignorance like this is what unconsciously helped me draft my unwritten entitlement of *insecurity validation* in my past relationships. I'm almost willing to bet that same ignorance has you wrapped up right now in drafting the identical thing to some capacity in your relationship. It might not be guest #4 that has you doing it, but trust and believe, it is one of them.

Nevertheless, before I get you to admit to yourself whichever guest you consistently invite, I first have to answer the burning question you probably want an answer for right now. You're probably asking: where did the need to be **reassured** come into play?

In case you didn't see it, let me further point it out for you. The roots of my family had such a strong hold on the core of my relationship foundation that eventually it sprouted into a mentality of being either selfish or weak in my past relationships.

Therefore, **reassurance** was needed because when I wasn't acting like an ASS by being selfish; I was acting an ASS by being weak. Remember we talked about this in the last section. It now should be coming to a head of why I used communication tactics such as "Assumptions and Speculations" and "Get Over It" in my relationships. The bottom line is I felt entitled to do so. Let's break this down even further!

In my mind, placing the insecurity of **reassurance** on my partner was my crazy way of placing accountability on my partner. I seriously believed placing nonsense accountability on my partner would ensure my partner would stay with me regardless of whatever actions I was giving to them at that time. I didn't know any better.

As stated before, the only thing I knew was my father's partners' stayed no matter the state of their relationship and my mother stayed no matter the state of her relationship. All I merely wanted was a repeat performance in my relationships.

What I failed to realize by wanting a repeat performance is that it would give me the audacity to feel entitled. I never knew desiring a repeat performance would cause me to place that type of nonsense accountability on my relationship partners. Of course looking back at that now, I question: who was I to feel so entitled? Who was I to feel my mate should nourish poisonous roots planted by my family? I had to really check myself, and guess what, people, YOU HAVE TO DO THE SAME!

Answer some serious questions for me right now. (Q1) Can you see how *insecurity validation* plays a part in failure of a relationship? (Q2) Can you see how *insecurity validation* can easily become one of your entitlements? While you thoroughly evaluate those questions, do something else for me. First, I want you to seriously ponder on everything you've read so far.

Second, I want you to add these two questions into the mix. (Q1) Who are you to feel so entitled? (Q2) Who are you to feel your mate should nourish and validate whatever guest you allow to draft your unwritten entitlements? When you finish honestly answering all those questions, follow up by asking, if you haven't already, if not unwanted guest #4, then which unwanted relationship guests do I constantly invite into my relationship that would give me a terrible entitlement such as *insecurity validation*?

While you do some digging to answer those questions, I'm going to continue telling you more about my past-unwritten entitlements. If nothing is coming to you, just keep questioning yourselves until an answer that makes you feel uncomfortable surfaces. That's when you will know that realness has entered the room. As I said before, my hope is the more unwritten entitlements I reveal to you, the easier it becomes for you to recognize your unwritten entitlements. With that said, let's move on!

YOU OWE ME

The next unwritten entitlement I had in past relationships was the *"you owe me"* entitlement. There are some of you right now that live by this *"you owe me"* entitlement in your relationship, but again don't even realize it. This entitlement is quite a doozy! It is a level above *insecurity validation*. In fact, if you're using this entitlement, which I'm sure most of you are, then God help us all, because you are definitely treading deep into ASS territory.

The *"you owe me"* entitlement is basically you convincing your partner that he/she *owes you* something for these imaginary sacrifices you've made in the relationship. Now, anybody that has been in a real relationship knows you have to make certain sacrifices for it to sustain, but, these sacrifices I'm talking about has nothing to do with the sacrifices a normal relationship needs to sustain. I'm referring to the sacrifices you think are sacrifices because your past relationship experiences led you to believe you were sacrificing something. **(One of the many faults associated with Guest #1)** Let me explain myself more in detail.

> **Transparency Moment:** I received the *"you owe me"* entitlement by mixing past relationships with an insane amount of ignorance and pinches of arrogance. I must say with honesty, what I'm about to reveal to you are not my proudest relationship moments, but definitely some of the most defining ones. This *"you owe me"* entitlement arrived by me somehow convincing myself I was doing extra in my past relationships. I had tricked myself (**manipulated myself**) into believing Shaun Upshaw was going above the call of duty. Yet again, here I was

being an ASS by convincing myself of my own BS. Remember we talked about this one.

Nonetheless, truth be told, I really wasn't doing anything extra or miraculous. The things I was doing in my relationships were supposed to be a given anyway. A mature person would see it as normal relationship duties and responsibilities. However, the keyword I said in that sentence is **mature.** Some quick examples of what I referred to as extra are: remaining faithful, considering my partner's feelings, listening to their problems, and hosts of other things you wouldn't believe I felt was extra. Let's just say that without a shadow of a doubt, I was immature, self-manipulated, and ignorant.

After reading that, I know you have questions. I'm sure one of the main questions is: how did you manage to transform what's supposed to be known relationship duties & responsibilities into a feeling of your partner owing you? Good question! The answer is I invited that pesky **(Guest #1)** into those particular relationships. I allowed it to enter into my space and throw me in a position to believe that somehow relationship duties & responsibilities were bonuses. I know that looks God awful to read, but this was my belief. Don't judge me!

The reason I felt that way, which by the way really isn't a legitimate reason, is some of my past relationships were riddled with so much infidelity, disrespect, and inconsideration that when I did manage to perform the known relationship duties & responsibilities with someone, I felt they owed me. The truth is I just never let go of those bad particular relationships that were riddled with all that negativity, which is why I felt so unconsciously entitled! Essentially, what I did was let my bad experiences penetrate and plant a mentality within me that I knew didn't make sense. I simply selected being an ASS to justify it over being a man to deal with the root of it. Can any of you relate?

I'm certain, my reason for having this entitlement is a little out there, but that was my truth. Based on the definition I've given you and reason for having this *you owe me* entitlement, the question is: do you have it? And before writing that question off with a quick NO ladies and gents, just keep in mind there are different reasons why you could unconsciously have it. In fact, one the reasons I hear so often regarding why people have this *you owe me* entitlement goes back to my favorite unwanted guest #4, which is roots of family.

> **Side Bar:** I hope by now you're seeing a pattern with this guest #4. As I stated in the beginning of this book, unwanted guest #4 is so powerful that it has the capabilities of weaving in and out of your relationship without you even realizing it. That is why it is so important you carefully gauge why you do what you do in your relationships. But moving on, in most cases, when I come across people that suffer from this *"you owe me"* entitlement, one of the underlining factors behind the feeling of their partner owing them usually reverts back to something to do with their mother or father.

For example, if a female has trust issues with her father, she may feel entitled that her partner owes her trust simply because that young lady hasn't dealt with the origin of her trust issues. Another example is, if a man never had a relationship with his mother, he might feel entitled that every woman owes him that motherly feel due to his mother not providing it. As a matter of fact, if I actually tried hard enough to pinpoint how guest #4 played more of a factor than guest #1 in my scenario, it's almost certain I could do it. That's just how serious this is people.

Now, we have reached the part in book again where I ask you do something for me. Don't worry! It's nothing life threating or anything. I simply want you to concentrate on the two unwritten entitlements I've given you up to this point. I want you to carefully assess my reasons for having those unwritten entitlements and try inserting my reasons into your situation.

Go ahead and try matching it up to see if anything I just said thus far sounds familiar to something you've done. Does it click yet? Are you or have you used either entitlement? Yes! No! Maybe!

Either way, keep in mind it doesn't have to look the way I did it. As stated, just keep questioning yourselves until that uncomfortable feeling arrives in the atmosphere. From there just welcome it in people.

Besides, I have two more shots at convincing you otherwise.

I pray these last two entitlements will assist you with discovering something you didn't know about yourselves. Maybe, just maybe one of these last two will finally flick the light on. It will hopefully allow you to comprehend on top of correcting whatever unwritten entitlements you have unconsciously given to yourself and unconsciously added to your relationship. My confidence is high!

NO LIFE OUTSIDE OF OURS

This entitlement will sound familiar once I begin to fully explain it to you. But basically, this entitlement is you feeling that your partner shouldn't have a life outside of the relationship life y'all share together. This specific entitlement might sound ridiculous to some of you, but some of you practically live by this entitlement in your relationship.

In fact, there are a mass amount of couples that unconsciously have this entitlement in their relationship. I have seen with my own two eyes both men and women use it. In my personal opinion, the factors that go into drafting this entitlement usually stem from some type of abandonment, control, and co-dependent issues. (**Unwanted guest #4**)

But of course, you know I use personal experience as my rule of thumb for evaluating everything. So having said that, let's jump right into why I believe you use it and why I had this deadly entitlement in my repertoire.

> **Transparency Moment:** This entitlement was something huge for me to let go. And to be honest, I recently just let go of it after my divorce a few years ago. One of the reasons it even became an entitlement in the first place was because I once again invited an unwanted guest into my relationship. This time it was guest #2, which is friends, also known as our advisors.

> Throughout the history of my past relationships, I had the habit of asking friends for relationship advice. It really hasn't changed much because I still ask for advice today, but the difference between then and now is my listening capacity. Meaning, there is only so far I will go with actually taking heed to the given advice. However, before I reached that level of

learning how to minimize what I should listen to regarding my relationship, I fell victim to bad advice. I allowed my friends to give their input on some key situations that shouldn't have been discussed with nobody other then the partner I was with at that time.

Unfortunately, I failed at doing so which in turn led to downfall after downfall in my relationships. Ultimately, what I'm saying here is I allowed my friends to impart this particular entitlement in me that eventually sprouted into something more negative than positive in my relationships. I allowed my friends to give me the idea that my partner shouldn't have a life outside of our relationship. I continuously let them pour into me this nonsense to believe my partner shouldn't have friends that are not my friends. They shouldn't go out without me, and they shouldn't make any plans without considering if I wanted to do it.

Clearly, this was some horrific advice given to me. Not only did this terrible advice cause me to transfer it from relationship to relationship, but it also caused me to lose a few relationships.

Some good relationships with great people, I might add. Matter of fact, just writing about it has me over here shaking my head in disgust, so I'm right along with you in your judgment of me right now. I am fully capable of taking accountability for my stupidity! What more can I say?

Now that my transparency moment is out of the way, let's dive into what's important, which is why I did it and why I think you do it. Upon some heavy soul searching, I have concluded there were two reasons why I decided to listen to that nonsense advice. The first and obvious reason was I thought my friends' advice had my best interest at heart. Here lies the joy of being naïve ladies and gentlemen because boy was I wrong. It wasn't until I fully comprehended what needs to be done with advice before implementing it, that I realized most of my friends' relationship advice came from a place of jealously or misery.

> **Side Bar:** Allow me to give you some considerations nobody ever gave me when it came to listening to friends' relationship advice.

<u>Three questions you should always ask before
implementing relationship advice from friends</u>

1. Who's giving the advice?
2. Why are they giving the advice?
3. Does the advice benefit them in any kind of way?

If you consider those three questions before accepting any relationship advice from a friend, it should reveal where their heart is in the matter. I didn't learn that until few years ago, but thank God it came when it did.

So there you have it. There is reason one. Now let's move on to reason two! The other reason why I listened to such poor advice was because my friends' advice came from a place of selfishness, which was good at that time. Let me explain why!

Their selfishness actually justified the selfishness that already existed in me regarding relationships. Fundamentally, what I'm saying is my friends provided me justification to release my selfish ways of thinking upon my relationship. At that time all I simply needed was some type of supportive reasons for indulging in my selfishness. I need a defense against common sense just in case it decided to pop in on me and try changing me. The point is those friends' practically provided me with more of a reason to continue being an ASS in my relationships.

The fact that I was constantly seeking ways to "Always Surrender Self" to my personal hang-ups concerning relationships made it easy for me to accept their advice. That's my truth people! Now what's yours? Can you admit to it? I believe you suffer from the same reason as me, which gives my reason for why I think you use it.

The truth is it doesn't matter whether you admit it out or not because anyone that believes his/her partner shouldn't have a life outside the relationship is truly experiencing selfish ignorance at its finest. There's absolutely no way a relationship will survive in that capacity. It is totally impossible. Here's why!

For two people to coexist in a real relationship, both of their needs, to feel some sort of personal independence in that relationship, has to be met for their personal <u>happiness</u> to be totally fulfilled. And secondly, no relationship can sustain any <u>healthiness</u> with one person in that relationship exercising a level of selfishness that forces his/her mate to ostracize their outside life to solely focus on the relationship life. That is by far beyond cockamamie.

If someone actually showed me a relationship like that and it actually worked, I would sign over my first born to that person. But, before I jump on my soapbox about that type of fraudulent couple, let me get back on track with my original point pertaining this particular entitlement. The *"No Life Outside Of Ours"* entitlement is terrible with no good in sight. There's simply no other way to explain it!

If there were any good that actually existed in this entitlement, I am almost certain it would come in the form of an opportunity, which is what I'm giving you right now. Here is your opportunity to face this entitlement head on and kick it out of your life for good. I believe you can do it! I did it!

So you have no excuse! You're actually in the right moment and with the right material to guide you out of this nonsense. Take advantage! Use my mistakes as a launching pad of what to avoid if you want to stay clear of entertaining a ridiculous entitlement such as *"No Life Outside Of Ours."*

Better yet, as previously stated, just continue to ask yourselves questions until the uncomfortable feeling of realness enters in. Remember, realness is the only friend you can possibly have at this point to save you. Take the help! Now, lets move on to discuss the final unwritten entitlement.

ULTIMATUMS

The last unwritten entitlement that crushed my past relationships was *ultimatums.* Some of you are probably wondering how did I manage to turn an *ultimatum* into an entitlement? Being that I'm on the outside looking in on all my past mistakes now, I must say it was quite easy to do. In fact, many of you are unconsciously doing it as well. Once I explain how this unfortunate thing occurred with me, you will have insight as to why you possibly do it.

> TRANSPARENCY MOMENT: Unwanted guest #3 was the primary suspect for the crime of transforming ultimatums into entitlements. I'm not ashamed to say that I once was one of those people that fell in love with seeing what people considered a perfect relationship. I even explained to you how it tainted my

communication in the previous section, so it's only befitting to inform you on how it gave me an unwritten entitlement.

By me inviting unwanted guest #3 into certain relationships, I basically gave control of my thoughts to whatever couple I was trying to emulate. If my woman at that time didn't act like the woman in the couple I was attempting to emulate, she was given an ultimatum. It was just that plain and simple. She either had to find a way to get on that level, or risk losing our relationship. That was just standard for me.

I unconsciously grew so accustomed to using this *ultimatum* that it unconsciously became a part of my relationship make-up. It was nothing for me to tell my partner that she should be like this woman or act like that woman. I know you're over there reading this in disgust wondering, how the hell did you get away with such nonsense? Well, for one reason I knew my money presented an <u>appeared</u> stability that most women fell victim to. (Remember we talked about the appearance of things in

"The Invitation" section so now you get the chance to see how it can be used against you)

With most of the women in my past relationships not having a clue of what the definition of true stability meant, it became natural to develop this entitlement. Honestly speaking, I didn't even know what true stability meant, which is another reason why I felt so entitled to us it. So, that's how I managed to transform an ultimatum into an unwritten entitlement.

It was certainly more immaturity on my part, but it was without a doubt ignorance on the part of my past relationship partners that accepted it. Truth of the matter is we both played the position of an ASS with this particular entitlement. I managed to find a way to Always Surrender Self to arrogance & immature behavior whereas my ex's found ways to Always Surrender Self to a false sense of stability & false perception of a real man. It was a sad state of affairs! There was no other way to put it! We were lost!

Okay! So, here is yet another transparent example of my past stupidity. Did it help you see some stuff? I asked because one thing I'm hopeful for is that these transparent moments are helping you. I hope my transparency is rendering clear understanding of how absurd it is to have not only this *ultimatum* entitlement, but also the other unwritten entitlements in your relationship. I want you to understand something for me ladies and gentleman. I'm not just out here putting myself on the chopping block to be judged. I'm putting myself out there with a goal of making you see your mistakes through mine. This particular unwritten entitlement does nothing to sustain the type of healthiness you desire in your relationship.

In fact, if this *ultimatum* entitlement has found its way into your relationship, then my advice is to just go cold turkey with using it. I say that because your audacity to request certain things to happen in your relationship will only grow bolder and more stupid. And once your mate concedes to that one *ultimatum*, your mind will unconsciously begin to tell you using *ultimatums* is how you get what you want out of your partner. Then you really will be setting yourselves up for failure once you adopt that attitude. Trust me!

At the end of the day, it is up to you to realize that *Ultimatums* or any other unwritten entitlement you may be unconsciously using is not designed for relationships, especially ones you want to last. As I stated before, if you want to know if you're using these unwritten entitlements, it requires some deep digging within self to discover it. Now, here is where I throw my shovel to the side for you to do the work now. Happy digging!

THE WRAP UP

I've showed you in the last section how inviting unwanted guests into your relationships taints your communication formulas. Now, I've just explained how inviting unwanted guests give you unwritten entitlements. It is decision time folks. If there is any ounce in you of wanting something different from failure in your relationships, I ask that you take an extreme serious look at yourselves to spot if what I've given thus far is accurate. Even if you think none of this applies to you, I would evaluate it just to be safe now rather than sorry later.

I told you in the introduction of this section that there is certain things in a relationship you're entitled to, but these unwritten entitlements do not fall under that category. These unwritten entitlements are results of carrying stuff that should have been let go of. These unwritten entitlements are unconsciously holding you down and costing you too many relationships. You must uproot and destroy this entitled way of thinking immediately because if you don't you are going to be mad at the wrong people for not having a successful relationship.

My question is why continue to allow your personal hang-ups, insecurities, selfishness, inconsideration, ignorance, and arrogance to fuel something that takes you to a nowhere destination. I want you to seriously ponder on that for a second. And add this significant nugget to your thoughts. Every characteristic I just named is an individual character flaw. Who better to correct those flaws then the person with them?

With that said, before we move on to the final bad characteristic associated with these unwanted guests, I want to leave you with a quote by Criss Jami. It states, "Man is not, by nature, deserving of all that he wants. When we think that we are automatically entitled to something, that is when we start walking all over others to get it."

As you turn the page and think about that quote, allow this last question to enter in. How many relationships are you willing to walk all over just to get a feeling of redemption that doesn't exist? My final plea is that you thoroughly evaluate yourselves! More importantly, be honest! Stop being afraid to allow that uncomfortable feeling of self-realness in because at this point it's nothing but self-realness that will break you free of ignorance.

VERSUS MINDSET

Congratulations! You are almost at the finish line! Can you feel yourself coming around the home stretch? Can you hear the crowd going wild? They're screaming your name and cheering for **YOU**. Although I cannot physically see it, I believe you are receiving everything I have revealed to you thus far about the characteristics of these unwanted guests. And I have confidence this information has caused you to pause and think about your actions in the past as well as present relationships. With that in mind, let's finish it strong!

To this point, I have given you the breakdown on how these unwanted guests taint your communication formula. I have given you the breakdown on how these unwanted guests give you unwritten entitlements. But now, I will render you the breakdown on how these unwanted guests give you a "*versus mindset.*" Before you utter one word, I know the question that is already hovering around your mental area. Shaun, what is a "*versus mindset?*"

A *"versus mindset"* is a mentality where your unwanted guest unconsciously initiates a **battle match** between your emotions, that in turn leads toward how you respond and act to relationship issues pertaining to you. I'm going to generalize here and say that most times you know the mature response and act to give when it comes to addressing a problematic situation in your relationship. But, instead of maturely offering that response free of interference from unwanted guests, you allow this *"versus mindset"* to determine which emotion should be your response and action. Rather than properly **balance** your emotions to reach a response and action that would help you better grasp your partner's issues with you, you unconsciously choose this *"versus mindset"* to do the dirty work for you.

For those of you that did not understand anything I just stated, let me give you a more concise explanation. The last thing I want to do is lose you so close to the end, especially with this *"versus mindset"* section having the potential to be the muddiest point in the book. So basically, a *"versus mindset"* is you choosing to be an ASS over the opportunity to listen, respond, and act in a way that sustains a healthy relationship. That is as clear-cut of a definition as it gets, ladies and gentlemen.

In a nutshell, this is yet another characteristic that's a hindrance to having a healthy relationship. If not careful and placed in check, this characteristic, like the others, will have you in more chaotic rather than peaceful situations in your relationship. So now that you're aware of the definition of a *"versus mindset,"* I must now provide you with the "**battle matches of emotions**" that your unwanted guest pushes into war against each other. Hopefully, after you read this section it will offer some insight as to why you most likely respond and act the way you do when your partner addresses you with problems regarding you. My fingers are certainly crossed for such a revelation. Nonetheless, let's jump right into this theory of mine.

After extensive observation mixed with personal experience of course, I believe there are three **battle matches of emotions** that unconsciously war within you whenever a relationship issue is presented to you and calls for self-evaluation. For the record, I'm aware of the array of emotions within us as humans, but I just believe there are only a few emotions that really need to be focused on when you respond and act in a relationship. The three **battle matches of emotions** are: Compromise vs. Combative, Common sense vs. Impulse, and Love vs. Fear. **Warning**: *From this point* *forward, make certain you pay close attention because I'm going somewhere with this!*

COMPROMISE VS. COMBATIVE

Whenever your relationship partner comes to you with an issue about you, this is the first **battle match** that is unconsciously set. Why? It's because whenever your partner comes to you with an issue regarding you, these two emotions would be considered the first responders to your partner's relationship emergency. And depending on what that issue might be, you tend to be uncertain rather than balanced on which side will do the responding. You tend to war with whether to be overly compromising or overly combative with your response. So rather than take time to maturely weigh in on the issue and balance those initial emotions to offer a proper response, you unconsciously enlist the services of this "*versus mindset.*"

> **Side Bar:** I'm not a licensed relationship therapist and based on my knowledge none of what I'm saying is documented in a phycology textbook. However, I am a man with a ton of mistakes on his relationship resume. I'm also a man that has carefully and thoroughly examined every fiber of those mistakes made in

my past relationships. So above all, what I'm asking you to do right now is just trust me! I know this might be hard to fathom for some, but I promise it will make sense once you decide to just open your mind up enough to receive it.

Getting back to the subject, this **battle match** between Compromise and Combative is what determines why you respond the way you respond to issues. It also determines the act that follows the response in the next match. Don't overthink it right now because I'll explain everything later and it will all come together by the end of this section. So just continue reading.

In this Compromise vs. Combative match, there are a few factors that determine which side prevails more often than none. Those factors are: (1) Your ability to listen and positively accept what's said about you vs. your ability to hear and negatively accept what's said about you (2) How deep of a stronghold the unwanted guest or guests roaming around your relationship have on you. (3) How well you actually know the person you are in relationship with. Here is my reason for believing this notion:

Transparency Moment: There were times when certain relationship partners would come to me with an issue concerning me and it wouldn't go too well. It wouldn't go well because my responses were combative 24/7. What normally would happen is instead of balancing my emotions to be more receptive to what that particular partner was attempting to do, I would respond in a combative manner to avoid listening to it. Now here is where you want to remember the factors I just told you about that will allow which side to prevail. It will help you understand this next part.

The reason I responded in a combative manner was to avoid listening. At that point in my life, I had already allowed my *"versus mindset"* to unconsciously choose being combative as the winning response almost every time. Why? Well, for one, I heard and negatively accepted what was said more often than listening and positively accepting what was being said about me regarding relationship issues.

Reason two for being so combative was the approach. Basically, I didn't like the way some of my partners would approach me with their issues. The reason why is their approach appeared as an exact replicate of my past experiences, which meant unwanted guest #1 was one of the guest that had control over this characteristic at that time.

And last, to be quite honest, I just would never properly balance my emotions to accurately judge the character of the person I was with. I simply grew comfortable with letting unwanted guest #1, which I just stated unconsciously controlled me, put them all in one box.

As a result of those three actions, I had began unconsciously carrying a combative tunnel vision into every relationship. Back then there was no such thing as a simple conversation with me. As stated before, I primarily had grown accustomed to tailoring all my responses to all problems pertaining to me in that combative manner. Deep down, the thing that transpired was I allowed my unwanted guests to overrule growth in those particular relationships and my "*versus mindset*" to choose my fate.

That right there is what being an ASS is all about people. It's about never improving self because you're too busy allowing your unwanted guest or guests to push you into **ALWAYS SURRENDEREING SELF**. It's about allowing self a constant reason to accept nonsense rather than welcome self-evaluation. But you already know that because I've been reminding you of it on just about every page in this book. Nevertheless, it wasn't until I finally became tired of my combative nature leaving me lonely that I welcomed a more balanced approach in this "Compromise vs. Combative" match. And fundamentally, you have to do the same if you're suffering from the same in your relationships. All right, that's enough about me. Let's get back on you.

Did that transparency moment remind you of anything you possibly could be doing or have done in your relationships? Do you find yourselves becoming combative when approached with issues that force you to evaluate yourselves? Or wait! Here is a twist. Do you find yourselves being more compromising when approached with issues that force you to evaluate yourselves?

Remember, you don't necessarily have to suffer in your relationship as I did by being combative 24/7. Your *"versus mindset"* can actually tip the scales in the other direction by causing you to be overly compromising with your responses to relationship issues. Surprise! Surprise! Surprise! You cannot forget that I'm just the example of transparency. Everything is totally up to you on how to implement yourself in these situations to see which side your *"versus mindset"* sways your responses.

But before you do that, let's briefly speak on being overly compromising because this is just as dangerous as being overly combative. As always, this emotion is a direct reflection of the unwanted guest or guests that control you. The same factors play a part. Nothing as far as that changes, but let's discuss how the dynamics of being overly compromising changes the situation.

> **Transparency Moment:** Know you're probably wondering how can I relate to being overly compromising when I just told you Shaun Upshaw suffered from being combative 24/7. And you are well within your right to have that thought, but you must have forgot one thing. I also said that you could suffer from inviting

multiple unwanted guests in any of these bad characteristics.

If you recall, I stated throughout every section that my favorite unwanted guest to invite into my relationships was #4, so you had to know this guest had some type of role to play in this characteristic. Let's talk about that role, shall we?

Although I told you unwanted guest #1 was my reason for being combative, I didn't mention the root of why I allowed unwanted guest #1 to make me combative in the first place. It ran deeper than just ex girlfriends with bad experiences.

If you recollect, I stated in the "Invitation" section that my mother stayed in her relationships despite evidence for a break up. Well, part of the reason for her doing that was she was overly compromising in her relationships. I witnessed it first hand. Here again, this is where you want to remember the factors that allow which side to prevail when the "*versus mindset*" is in full effect. In case you forgot, I will apply them here to refresh your memory. Let me give you a breakdown!

My mother suffers daily because of something that happened to her growing up pertaining to relationships. (**Unwanted Guest #4**) From my understanding, my grandmother left my mother along with her sibling with my grandfather to be raised by him without a valid reason. To this day my mother is affected by my grandmother's actions and refuses to let that situation go. Whatever that did to my mother clearly lingered into her relationships as an adult, which caused her to hear and negatively accept whatever issues were brought up to her about her in relationships.

Rather than balance her emotions to properly respond to those issues brought up to her about her, she permitted her unwanted guest to cause her "*versus mindset*" to choose overly compromising as the clear-cut winner in every Compromising vs. Combative match. Why? Simple! She didn't want to experience what she experienced growing up, which was being left alone for no apparent reason.

So, rather than evaluate the character of the person she was with to check the validity of their issues with her, she unconsciously permitted unwanted guest #4 to let her "*versus mindset*" choose overly compromising as her response every single time. Why? As I stated before, she just didn't want to experience what she experienced growing up. Do you now see how those factors play a role in which side prevails? Can you see the pattern here?

I hope so because that's enough with discussing my mother's issues. This book was not written to expose her behavior. It was written to introduce you to you, but through me. Although she is a part of me, she will have to go through this same process as you once she reads the book to evaluate if my theories are accurate. With that stated, I know your next question probably is: Shaun, how does her story correlate with you being overly compromising in your relationships when you initially stated you were combative?

Simple! I told you in the "Invitation" section about the unfortunate circumstance of both my parents' traits rubbing off on me. Well, now you see the unwanted gift I unconsciously received from my mother. My mother unconsciously put her relationship fears on me, which unconsciously forced me to place them on my relationships. The reason I transformed into being overly combative was because I quickly grew tired of my relationship partners walking all over me from starting out as overly compromising. I grew irritated with the whole give & take aspect of my past relationships in which I was doing all the giving because I didn't want them to leave me for no apparent reason.

So instead of just evaluating my mess to discover that unwanted guest #4 was the original culprit, I allowed it to invite another guest, which was guest #1. And ultimately that brought along this "*versus mindset*" to make all my emotional responses for me. For a long time, I did not exercise any **balance** with my emotions. I just knew how it felt to be overly compromising and figured being overly combative was the best solution for my responses from that point moving forward.

By doing that, the one thing I didn't realize is not having **balance** with my emotions to respond in a mature way was the reason my relationships often failed. I had to figure that part out on my own. Now, there's some realness for you. The question now is: Could the same be happening to you? I don't know, but remember, honesty is your best friend when answering real question such as that one!

So while you assess that question along with everything else you've just read, I want you to comprehend that here lies yet another transparency moment that directly explains why implementing balance in this first match for a response is significant. Everything I have just given you should be enough to show why you cannot continue to allow unwanted guest or guests along with an associate like the "*versus mindset*" to control your responses. The bottom line is, as long as you permit unwanted guest or guests to initiate a war to respond to relationship issues regarding you, nothing but chaos, misunderstanding, and friction within you and your relationship will ensue.

You will always be in a position where your emotions are not balanced nor controlled by the maturity needed to sustain a relationship. Your emotions will always be haunted by the circumstances you refuse to face and correct. What I want you to do right now is simply take a moment to absorb everything you've just read. Whether you believe it or not, this was a ton of information to consume in these small amounts of pages. And if you are anything like myself, I know you probably want to sit and reflect to see if it applies, which is cool.

My prayer is that everything you just read didn't go over your head because it wasn't broken down clearly enough. Or worse. It went in one ear and out the other because you refuse to thoroughly evaluate to see if it applies. Either way I will say this, if you don't strongly consider everything I just revealed as a potential threat, then you're a bigger ASS than I assumed. I say that because this information should at least make you want to dig within self to see if any of this theory holds truth.

As always, all you have to do is just be open to trying it. While you hopefully make your attempts at trying, I will be moving on to discuss the next **emotional match**.

COMMON SENSE VS. IMPULSE

Whichever side of the Compromise vs. Combative match your "*versus mindset*" chooses as an initial response will determine the winner of this Common Sense vs. Impulse match. This match is what provides the unconscious emotional <u>ACT</u> that follows the unconscious emotional <u>RESPONSE</u> from the Compromise vs. Combative match. You might want to reread that a few times to comprehend it because I'm not ashamed to admit I had to and I'm the one who wrote it. But jokes aside, an example would be say you're a person that instead of balancing your emotions for a mature response, you allow your "*versus mindset*" to push you into being overly compromising. If that is the case, the unconscious emotional <u>ACT</u> that follows the decision of being overly compromising is being impulsive. It's vice versa with being overly combative as well.

Does that make sense? If not, do me a favor and define impulsive for me then. Matter of fact, I will make it easy for you. The definition of impulsive is acting or done without forethought. Last time checked anything done without forethought most certainly lacks common sense. Think about it for a second. If you're overly combative or compromising rather than **balanced** with your emotions when an issue is brought up to you about you, what other emotion can you <u>ACT</u> out of other than impulse. Anybody that says differently is lying from the pits of the lying den.

Transparency Moment: In the relationships where I was being overly combative, my <u>ACTS</u> that followed most certainly lacked forethought. With hindsight being 20/20, I fully recognize now the intent of those women who came to me with issues about me at that time. The majority of them wanted nothing but growth for our relationship. However, due to unwanted guest #1 having control over that combative side and my *"versus mindset"* choosing the side my unwanted guest unconsciously told it to, I couldn't see it, which is why I continuously permitted the impulsive side of my acts to outweigh the common sense side.

The same applies when I started out being overly compromising in certain relationships. Those <u>ACTS</u> that followed lacked forethought as well. By me not having a true sense of my identity, being overly compromising with my response lead to me being impulsive with my actions. It was easy for me to trick myself into believing those women had my best interest at heart in spite of what their actions displayed. I was more focused on compromising to stay in unhealthy relationships versus balancing my emotions to see if those relationships meant me no good.

What I'm basically saying in both scenarios is since I lacked balance with my initial emotional response, there was no way the side of common sense could be activated. How could it be? If I wasn't being overly combative by not listening, I was selling myself short by being overly compromising. So how can impulsive acts not be spawned from any of those responses? But, nevertheless, the most important question here is: Are you making the same mistake?

In all honesty, either scenario in that transparency moment could be unconsciously happening to you right now in your relationships. Your responses could be leading you to operate out of impulse instead of common sense. This is something you have to evaluate for yourselves. The truth of the matter is impulsive actions are what have a lot of you in a position to not see the truth about yourselves. It's blocking common sense from entering so that you can see the truth about your relationship as well.

What it boils down to is **balance** needs to implemented in every facet of your responses to relationship issues for the act of common sense to play a part. If not, the winning emotion of this Common Sense vs. Impulse match won't provide the results you need to sustain a relationship. The results will not give you **balanced** common sense responses. Impulse will be your winner and your relationship will be the loser. It's your choice people!

But although it is your choice, if I were you in your shoes, I would want my control back. I would want common sense to be at the forefront so that my actions would have forethought. I would want to stop this ASS behavior by allowing this "*versus mindset*" to fight my battles. Moreover, I would desire to know how to properly respond and act to future issues about me in my relationships. But again, it's your choice! Let's move forward!

LOVE VS. FEAR

Although this is the last battle match of emotions you encounter, this Love vs. Fear match is the most significant of all three. This emotional match is the root of the battle, whereas the first two matches are the trunk and branches.

Basically, this match is what fuels everything. Let me give you a recap. The Compromise vs. Combative match is the initial emotional response. The Common Sense vs. Impulse match is the acts that follow the initial response. However, this Love vs. Fear match is the primary reasoning, outside of your unwanted guests, of why this "*versus mindset*" exists in the first place.

This is the match that helps you discover what drives your responses and actions. This is the indicator match that reveals if your responses and acts are given out of love or fear. If you can figure that out, then you have come across the very reason you respond the way you respond along with the reason for your acts that follow that response. You get one step closer to discovering that one side of this match promotes growth through sacrifice whereas the other side fosters stagnation through being an ASS.

But, before you can reach that plateau of realness, you must first discover the distinction between love and fear in a relationship. Why? Some of you have made the mistake of intertwining the meanings of these two words. Some of you have confused these emotions to a point where you mistakenly believe you're operating in love, but in reality you're maneuvering in fear. Do you remember what I said about <u>FEAR</u> in the preface? If not, bookmark this page right now and go back to read it. After you read the preface again, it will begin to make sense. Now go ahead. I will be here waiting on you.

1 Mississippi, 2 Mississippi, 3 Mississippi…Okay, Welcome back! I know some of you didn't even bother reading the beginning and it's good. But I want to give kudos to those who did because it shows you're committed to getting a better grasp on understanding this part of the section. But anyway, whether you read it or not, I'm going to give you the part I want your focus on. The only reason I'm doing it is because I want everyone to understand where I'm coming from with this part of the section.

The preface states "Fear is the one word that keeps you from succeeding in your relationships. It's **<u>fear of hurt</u>**,

fear of rejection, and **fear of self-exposure** that hinders you. The very thought of fear is the reason you are unable to face yourselves to see the real problem. In fact, it's fear that leaves you in relationship rut after relationship rut. Without a doubt, fear keeps you from transforming into an ideal mate purposed for sustaining a healthy relationship."

I chose that part of the preface because **FEAR** is the key element that triggers your responses and actions. It's fear of not wanting to go through the same cycle of hurt that keeps you from balancing your emotions to respond and act in a manner that sustains a relationship. It's fear that creates an easiness for you to shift the responsibility to the "*versus mindset*" to choose a response and act for you. Moreover, it's fear that keeps every unwanted guest or guests in your relationships unturned, undeclared, and untamed. Fear is 100% destroying you! Shaun, how did you get over relationship fear?

> **Transparency Moment:** I got rid of fear by simply choosing not to be afraid anymore. What? Yeah, you read it right! I got rid of fear by simply choosing not to be afraid anymore. I decided to just put myself back out there as if

nothing ever happened in my past. I realized that to fully operate out of love in your relationship, you don't have room for fear. But besides that, loneliness began to take its toll on me. I grew tired of not having someone to share my life goals and ambitions with. I grew tired of the entire break up process. I grew tired of having that failure over my head.

Instead of creating excuses, I chose solutions. I knew that in order for me to get the answers needed to sustain a relationship, I had to dig deep within me to get them. Once I dug deep for those answers, I realized that back then my fear to love outweighed the act of love I desired to give in my relationships. I comprehended that fear to let myself love was the root of why I allowed the unstableness of my past to sabotage my responses and actions. I came to grips that fear to love prevented me from properly balancing my emotions to respond and act in a manner that sustained a relationship. The bottom line is I feared that Shaun Upshaw wasn't good enough to possess a healthy relationship.

How many of you suffer from that same fear? How many of you have convinced yourselves of the nonsense that relationships are just not for you? How many of you have let good people leave your life because you allowed your fear to love to outweigh the act of love you desire to give in your relationship? You don't have to be ashamed to admit it. In fact, admitting to it is the first step toward releasing that fear so that you are in position to finally love the way you desire to love in your relationships.

This emotional battle of Love vs. Fear is a serious battle, ladies and gentlemen. This match could be the difference in you living as the best YOU in a relationship vs. maintaining a YOU just to be in a relationship. I don't know about you, but just maintaining in a relationship is not something I would want to do. Who the hell just wants to go through the motions of a relationship with no chance to grow? The time is now to stop this mess people. Your relationships are suffering from the fact that you refuse to let go of your unwanted guests and balance your emotions to make mature choices.

Your inability to choose love has allowed this "versus mindset" to take over your entire emotional decision making, which by the way doesn't benefit you. Fear will literally ruin any chance of you loving to your full capability in a relationship. Fear will have you continuously inviting your unwanted guest into relationship after relationship. Fear will unconsciously end your relationship before it ever begins. With that said, my questions to you are: How long will you allow fear to paint the outcome of your relationships? How long will you use fear as a navigation tool to reach a destination of failure? Lastly, how long will fear outweigh your desire to love the person you're in a relationship with unconditionally?

If you want my advice, I advise you to wake up and make provisions that place you in a position to choose LOVE!

THE WRAP UP
Of course I cannot speak for you, however I will say this to you. As I was writing this section, everything began to mentally open up for me as to why I once responded and acted in a specific manner toward relationship issues regarding me. As stated in the beginning, I really cross my fingers with hope that reading this section has done the same for you.

If it has not done that for you then let me offer a brief synopsis of what happens when you decide to let go of your way of thinking to better understand the information you just read. Maybe that will help along the process!

Once you decide to let go of personal mess, there is this feeling that you get within you. And I must admit that the feeling is very eye opening. It is a feeling of self-discovery. Once you reach that point of discovering your make-up as an individual and how it affects your relationship, you see everything under a new light.

What used to be problems magnified by you to spotlight your partners' issues now becomes a deep evaluation of how you contributed to it. More important, you start to view self-discovery as a prime opportunity to better yourselves in every face of life, especially relationships. To a degree, self-discovery is a second chance at life.

How is that Shaun? Why do you think it goes to that level? Well, it wasn't until I realized how deep and mental everything pertaining to relationships go that I better understood this entire "*versus mindset*" concept. Basically, to understand what you've just read and process it to a point where it begins to make sense, you literally must step outside of everything you have unconsciously built around you as protection. You must recognize that what you've so-called 'built as protection from hurt' isn't really protecting you. It's actually hurting you! It's stopping your relationship progress. Check this out!

Relationships are deep in nature. There is nothing surface about coming together with another person to form something you desire to remain healthy and sustainable for years to come. You have to do some serious soul searching to unnerve everything your past hang-ups have forced you to buy into and accept concerning relationships. You have to seriously want something different for yourselves. You have to reject the entry of failure at all cost. More significantly, you have to want a healthy relationship bad enough to try something new.

That said here's your first shot at it! What are you going to do with it?

LUXURY WITH NO MAINTENANCE

What are your thoughts right now on everything? I really wish we could talk about it face-to-face because I know you have so much to tell me. You know one thing I had hoped for with writing this book was that your mind didn't get overloaded. That surely wasn't my intention. My goal was to actually just challenge you. Question your motives and actions in relationships!

Whether that happened or not, here is the crux of this entire book. It reminds me of this story about a friend of mine. One day this friend and me were sitting around talking and she said to me, "Shaun, I want a BMW so bad that it haunts my dreams." After she gave me that comparison, I was inclined to believe she really wanted that car. Needless to say, she finally got her wish and purchased her ultimate driving machine. She drove that car everywhere with a huge smile of confidence on her face, that is until that maintenance light flashed yellow.

After taking her BMW to the service department for the first time, her smile of confidence quickly transformed into a look of disgust once the bill arrived. To make a long story short, the car continued to give her problem after problem. Eventually she sold it because she couldn't afford to keep up with the maintenance. From there, she went from an ultimate driving machine back to the vehicles she drove before purchasing that BMW.

Now I told you that story for a few reasons. Like my friend that desired a BMW so bad that it haunted her dreams, here sits you wanting the same, but just in a different form. Instead of a car, you want a successful relationship. So what do you do? As my friend did, you build enough confidence to fulfill that want, but you never take into consideration the same thing my friend didn't take into consideration, which is are you in a position to afford the maintenance that comes along with that luxury? You never take time to evaluate if you're fully ready for the responsibility.

The overall point is, most of you want the luxury of a relationship because it looks and feels good, but you never want to perform the duties it requires for you to maintain it. You never want to check yourselves to see if you are mentally ready to dive into such a commitment until you are already in the commitment. So then, what do you do? I will be glad to tell you! Instead of being uncomfortable to evaluate what it really takes on your end to maintain the luxury of a relationship, you prematurely trade in that relationship for another one or even worse, go back to what you know best, which is a poor mentality, insecurities, and hang-ups that your unwanted guest provided you about relationships.

What it comes down to is if you want the luxury of a relationship ladies and gentlemen, you have to pay for it. You have to know the cost for maintaining it. More significantly, you need the tools and resources to sustain it when problems arrive. As you turn the page to receive your wake up call, I want you to honestly evaluate yourselves to see if you have what it takes to sustain a relationship. The reason I want an honest assessment is because this wake-up call is going to provide the reasons you need to break-up with these unwanted guests and the characteristics attached to them. The only way you can fully receive it though is by getting in position to acknowledge, accept, and associate the core issues with your failures. Just accept the task!

By the way, thank you for giving me the opportunity to offer my insight on relationships. It was my pleasure to be this transparent with you. I must admit it further helped me to realize more things I need to change about myself while writing this book. But anyway, the last thing I want to say to you is: a relationship will not flourish until you become real about your downfalls. It will not give you what you desire until you recognize the part you play in it.

What better day to start learning this information about yourselves then today? The sooner you start the process, the closer you get to possessing that healthy relationship you always desired.

WAKE UP CALL

Dear Reader,

I f you ever stayed in a city with horrible winter conditions, I'm sure you've seen potholes before and probably experienced running into a few. The potholes where I'm from were massive and very capable of damaging your vehicle at any given time. Even when the city would "fix these potholes" once the weather broke, the terrible road conditions never changed. I recall one day driving slowly over a road of what the city considered "fixed potholes" and asking myself why does it seem as if these roads with "fixed potholes" look and feel even worse than it did prior to fixing.

I was literally confused about that scenario. So I did the next logical thing to do when you want answers about something, which is research it. During my research, I learned quite a bit about potholes. I learned that potholes are formed by the expansion and contraction of ground water that enters under the pavement. I learned how small potholes become huge potholes. And outside of all the other scientific technical stuff, I also learned why my city's so-called "fixed potholes" made the road look and feel even worst than the road prior to fixing.

Based on my research, it would appear the city was more concentrated on temporary patching rather than using a more permanent solution for fixing the pothole problem. Apparently, to temporarily patch a road cuts down on time and money whereas using a more permanent solution is time consuming and dollar driven. A permanent solution would call for workers to focus more on restructuring the entire perimeter of a pothole for it to blend back in with the pavement whereas temporary patching doesn't require such detailed work.

Now, if you're sitting there wondering how does potholes correlate with a relationship book, then let me tell you. Basically, you have allowed these unwanted guests along with their attached bad characteristics of communication, entitlements, and mentalities to place huge potholes on your relationship roads. You have let all the nonsense of your unwanted guests get you (**mad**) to expand and (**bitter**) to contract negativity, hang-ups, and fear under your heart.

Rather than perform a permanent solution to fix the problem once and for all by restructuring the entire perimeter surrounding your initial hurt, you select temporary solutions to patch your core issue. Rather than take your time and learn just what it is that keeps your relationships failing, you cut corners and ignore it. Essentially, what happens is instead of thouroghly self-evaluating, you re-patch and re-patch and re-patch until your road appears smooth enough for someone new to travel on it again. Then with no remorse, you permit that someone to place something as valuable as his or her heart over your re-patched relationship road that you refuse to correctly fix. That, ladies and gentlemen, is what ultimately makes you an ASS, not just a person that Always Surrender Self, but a natural ASS in the true definition.

Before you chose to pick up this book and read it, you had full-blown deniability concerning these unwanted guests and their associates. But now that you've reached this part of the book, you should know that all deniability has gone right out the window. You should know that your crutch of saying your actions were unconscious no longer exists. The accountability for your actions finally rests where it belongs. Accept it!

I know this isn't an easy process. I told you that earlier in the book. But if you desire real progress in your relationship, you should worry less about the complexity of the process and more about just starting it, especially if you're experiencing anything close to what I revealed and experienced in my past relationships. At this very point, the worst thing you can do is to continue discarding relationships and transferring your mess to other relationships. Why?

Eventually, you will run out of fingers to point. You will run out of corners to hide in. You will run out of mirrors to avoid. And finally you will run out of people who are willing to be in a relationship with you. Well, how does that happen? The faults you refuse to correct about yourselves become evident. That is how it happens.

The question of "why you can't sustain a relationship?" begins to form. Basically, your cover is now blown! But, here's a solution if you care to listen! I think the best way to avoid being exposed is by being real upfront about who you are and where you are personally with your journey in life. In my humble opinion, the best way to shy away from nonsense is by just dealing with it head on.

Listen people, at the end of the day, all I want for you is a clean slate, which is something everybody deserves in a relationship. In fact, the chance for a clean slate is one reason I even wrote this book in the first place. I just didn't write it for you to judge my mistakes. I wrote this book because I believe in relationships. I believe in love. I believe in people!

I take my calling as an author seriously and believe that through my faults, others will feel compelled to reveal their faults. I finally comprehend that my relationship ignorance wasn't in vain. It's now realized that I am a walking example of past mistakes here to serve as guide for what to avoid. My past relationship ignorance is my gift to you so that you can break the shackles these unwanted guests, along with its attached bad characteristics, have placed on your life.

Accept it as my gift to you people. All I want is for you to be in position to identify the perpetrators that have robbed you of the happiness you desire in your relationships. I just want to these expose unwanted guests along with their tainted communication formulas, unwritten entitlements, and versus mindsets. I merely want to contribute to you finding the light needed for you to walk out of darkness. But before all that happens, you need **to break up with everything that hinders you.** And hopefully this book has provided you the blueprint on **why** you should do it and **how** you should do it.

Whether you know it or not, this book is the **closure** you need to move forward with experiencing relationship life as it should be experienced, which is with joy, peace, and love. Fundamentally, I have given you a playbook filled with my mistakes so that you can recognize yours and no longer have to be involved with ASS behavior. You should use this information and use it wisely, ladies and gentlemen.

Do you remember when I asked you in the beginning of this book to let me prove that I was here for you? Well hopefully, you see it now! And from this point moving forward, I want you to question what drives your relationship, challenge what doesn't make sense within it, remove what doesn't add to it, and apply a new you in it. If you at least take some seriousness in that process, I bet everything will begin to unfold and begin to make sense to you.

One last thing before I forget: To those of you that read and understood the purpose of this book then congrats on receiving a way to **<u>BREAK UP WITH ASS BEHAVIOR</u>**! For those of you that read and didn't understand the purpose of this book, then I don't know what to tell you other than good luck with your attempts at sustaining a relationship. By no means am I saying that this is the relationship bible for sustaining a healthy relationship. However, what I am saying is if you didn't learn at least something from this book, you're a bigger ASS than I assumed and you need to <u>WAKE UP</u>. Be blessed!

Respectfully,

A former ASS

Shaun D. Upshaw

www.ingramcontent.com/pod-product-compliance
Lightning Source LLC
Chambersburg PA
CBHW060306050426
42448CB00009B/1754